How to Fly an Airliner

A Concise Guide...

Author: John Pullen

Copyright © 2013 John Pullen

ISBN: 9781497552715

Publisher: John Pullen

All rights reserved. No part of this publication may be reproduced, stored in a retrieval system or transmitted in any form or by any means, electronic, mechanical, photocopying, recording or otherwise, without the prior written permission of the copyright owner of this book.

First EBook Edition: 2013

First Print Edition: 2014

Printed by CreateSpace, An Amazon.com Company

Cover Image Design: JPP

Available from Amazon.com, CreateSpace.com and other retail outlets

www.johnpullenwriter.com

To

Tony, Stephen, Margaret,

Tina, Mark

and remembering Pat

Contents

Introduction   11

Chapter 1: How a Plane Flies   15

Lift, Weight, Thrust and Drag

Main Flight Controls

Chapter 2: Flight Planning   23

Choosing the Best Route

Weather

Fuel Requirements

Weight and Balance

Chapter 3: Pre-Flight Preparation   41

Arrival at the Aircraft

The Walk-Round

The Cockpit

Ground Operations

Chapter 4: Start-Up and Taxi   59

The Jet Engine

Pre-Flight Systems Checks

Engine Start and Push-Back

Taxi to the Runway

Chapter 5: Take-Off and Climb   85

Take-Off Run

Climb to Cruising Level

Chapter 6: En-Route Flight   93

Passenger Services

Navigation

Radio Communications

Chapter 7: Descent   107

Initial Descent

Initial Approach

Chapter 8: Landing 113

Final Approach

Landing

Arrival and Deplaning

Chapter 9: Aircraft Data 123

Further Information 131

Contacts

Other Books by the same Author

Introduction

In today's world many people have flown aboard an airliner. Some love it, a few hate it or feel apprehensive about flying in general and many feel it is an experience with positives and negatives which they have to undergo in order to get to their intended destination.

Perhaps the biggest flaw in their experience is the fact that they feel they have no control over their movements. Once you reach the airport you lose control over much of what you can choose to do. Your bags are taken away from you and you sometimes wonder if you'll ever see them again. You are screened and checked, moved to a departure room and then wait to board a metal tube which takes you miles up into the air.

Any weather problems that you encounter such as turbulence have to be endured by staying in your allocated seat. And your only contact with what is going on is either from the busy cabin crew or the disembodied voice of the pilot coming over the intercom now and again and giving you a few snippets of information.

It's no wonder that most feel they have no control or understanding about what really goes on. And that is what this book aims to change. We will take you through a typical flight from the preparation that has to be done before the pilot even goes aboard the aircraft, through all the phases of a flight until it reaches its destination.

In most cases, if you understand what is going on you can relax and enjoy your flight much more. And you will know that flying really is the safest form of travel you can take.

Finally, there are many who have dreamed of becoming an airline pilot. And for the great majority it will remain just a dream. But by the end of this book you will have a good idea of what it really takes to be the captain of a modern airliner; the responsibilities, tasks and expertise required of both the captain and first officer.

If you would like to go further into aviation and learn how to fly a light aircraft such as a Piper Warrior, one of the world's leading pilot training planes, then you should check out "How to Fly a Plane" by John Pullen which is also available direct through Amazon & CreateSpace and other outlets.

"There is an art to flying.

The knack lies in learning to throw yourself

at the ground and miss…"

Douglas Adams

Chapter 1

How a Plane Flies

Lift, Weight, Thrust and Drag

There are four main forces acting on an aircraft. They are Lift, Weight, Thrust and Drag. To be able to take off an aircraft needs to generate lift by moving down the runway. The engine provides the power which is termed thrust and this is translated into forward speed. As the speed increases the wing develops lift.

But why does a wing generate lift?

The answer lies in the shape of the wing. If you look at a typical wing in cross-section which is called an airfoil, you will see that the upper surface is more curved than the lower surface.

When air passes over the airfoil, the air passing over the upper side has to travel further than the air on the lower side. This means that it also has to travel faster. The result is that a pressure difference occurs between the two surfaces. With low pressure on the upper wing and high pressure on the lower wing, lift is generated. When take-off speed is reached, it means that the thrust is sufficient to generate enough lift to overcome the aircraft's weight. The aircraft takes off.

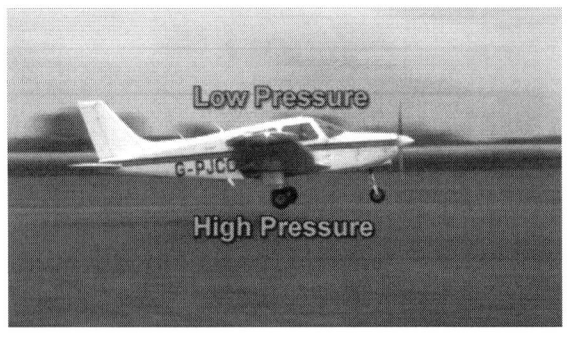

The airfoil shape of the wing generates lift

If we now take a look at the aircraft once it is straight and level flight or in the cruise, we can see how the same four forces act on the plane. They are the aircraft's weight which acts vertically downwards. Lift which as we have just seen is generated in the wings. Thrust is the forward motion of the aircraft and is powered by the engine. Finally there is drag which acts in the opposite direction to thrust and is caused by air friction.

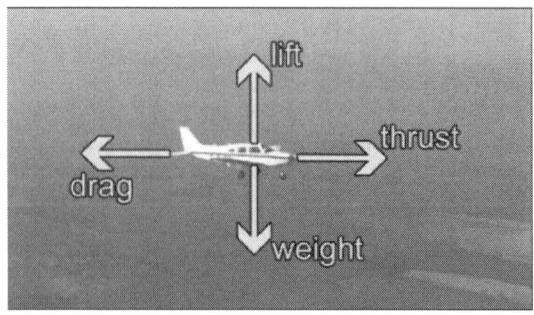

In straight and level flight, all forces are in balance

In straight and level flight, lift balances weight and thrust balances drag. The aircraft is said to be in equilibrium. If for any reason the aircraft should go out of equilibrium such as by turning or by changing engine power, the pilot will use his flying controls to bring the aircraft back into balance.

These forces apply to all aircraft whether it is a light aircraft such as the one illustrated above or a Boeing 747-400 series airliner weighing close to 390 tonnes.

Main Flight Controls

No matter how big or complicated an aircraft is, it is controlled and manoeuvred using two primary flight controls which in turn affect three main flying surfaces. Movement of these control surfaces allow the aircraft to change its attitude. The flight controls are the control column which many years ago was called a "joystick" and the rudder pedals.

Now the attitude of an aircraft can be expressed in terms of three axes which pass through its centre of gravity. By manipulating the aircraft around these axes, we can cause it to pitch up and down, to roll left or right and to yaw to the left or right. Let's take a look at each of these and observe the effect they have.

Movement around the lateral axis is called pitching and pitch is controlled by the elevators using the control column

The lateral axis is an imaginary line in the direction of wing tip to wing tip and passes through the aircraft's centre of gravity. To utilise this axis, the pilot will push the control column forwards or bring it back. This causes the elevators on the tail-plane to move and the aircraft to pitch up or down.

The longitudinal axis is a line drawn through the length of the aircraft and passing through its centre of gravity. When the control column is turned or operated to the left or right it causes the ailerons located on the trailing edge of the wings to move, which in turn rolls the aircraft left or right.

Movement around the longitudinal axis is called rolling and roll is controlled by the ailerons using the control column

Therefore, both pitch and roll are controlled by the pilot using the control column. The final change of attitude is yawing and this is controlled by the rudder at the back of the tail-plane using the rudder pedals which the pilot operates with his feet. If the left rudder pedal is pushed forward, the plane will yaw to the left and vice versa. This time the axis passes vertically down through the aircraft and like the others, through its centre of gravity. It is known as the normal axis.

Movement around the normal axis is called yawing and yaw is controlled by the rudder using the rudder pedals

There are many other ways in which a pilot can influence and affect the attitude of an aircraft's flight, such as the use of the throttle levers, deploying flaps, using air brakes and raising or lowering the landing gear or undercarriage. We shall investigate these as we continue our flight.

"The optimist invents the aeroplane.

The pessimist invents the parachute…"

George Bernard Shaw

Chapter 2

Flight Planning

Choosing the Best Route

So we've covered some of the basics behind how a plane flies and how it is manoeuvred by the pilot. But as we start our lead-up to this flight, there is still a lot to do before the crew even board the aircraft. Planning is essential in most things and flying a jet is no exception.

The internet is an integral part of our lives and it has made a difference in how the captain of our airliner may first check out our up and coming flight. A couple of hours before arriving at the departure airport, he or she may log in to their airline flight planning department and take a look at the proposed flight plan. This is likely to have been produced about four hours before departure time.

The factors involved in choosing a particular route will often have a bottom line of what is the most cost effective. Time in the air and fuel management are crucial in keeping an airline financially secure, so every effort is made to make the flight cost effective. The flight plan will have been filed with the first Air Traffic Control Centre (ATCC) on route and from there passed to other centres further down the route.

Other factors that will have been taken into account are Air Traffic Control (ATC) charges for using their airspace and services. The weather will have been checked to see if any adverse conditions are likely to affect the flight.

Headwinds can cause the aircraft's speed over the ground to slow up and therefore spend longer in the air.

Tailwinds will have the opposite effect. We will look at the weather in more detail in the next section.

The dispatcher will also have checked what are known as NOTAMS. These stand for Notices to Airmen and are produced by the different air authorities along the route. They usually cover temporary factors that may affect the flight.

These can range from a navigational beacon being under repair, military exercises which may close particular areas and airport closures. The latter is important as alternate airports are always available if it becomes necessary to change the final destination for any reason.

NOTAMS are also used in the UK to denote when a flight carrying a member of the Royal Family is taking place. Other aircraft are kept clear of this route which is termed a Purple Airway.

All of these details are brought together with the projected load sheet (more of this later) and engineering reports as to the serviceability of the particular aircraft into what is termed the flight briefing package. This all means that the captain will have a good idea of what to expect about the coming flight before even leaving for the airport.

Weather

We have already mentioned the subject of headwinds and how they can slow an aircraft's groundspeed. We also touched on tailwinds, which means that the aircraft's speed over the ground is increased and this is looked on by all concerned as a good thing.

All pilots are trained and qualified in meteorology, so they are able to interpret weather charts and reports produced by the meteorological centres. The weather consists of a constantly changing set of factors which can produce a whole host of conditions along a route. Luckily, modern airliners are able to fly safely above most weather conditions.

But they must take-off, climb, descend and land in the weather conditions current at that time in that particular location. However, if conditions are "below minima" which means it is unsafe for a landing, the aircrew will divert to another airport with better weather conditions. In this day and age with modern equipment, this is quite unusual but does happen. Once again, this will have been planned for and be in the flight plan.

The atmosphere through which an aircraft flies is constantly changing and those changes lead to many types of weather phenomena. All of these will affect a flight in one way or another. Let's take a look at some of these now.

Temperature

One of the reasons why air masses move around is due to changes in temperature. The action of the sun is to heat up the air near the ground which then rises. This rising air is replaced by cooler air and a circulation pattern is set up. However, the air that rises becomes cooler the higher it gets. It also expands until it reaches a level where the temperature is the same. The rate of cooling of dry air is about three degrees Celsius for every one thousand feet in height.

If the air has enough moisture in it, it may eventually reach a point called its Dew Point and at this stage the air is said to become saturated. Now if further cooling of the air happens, clouds will form in the atmosphere. This has an effect on the rate of cooling with height, so an average is usually given which is about two degrees Celsius per thousand feet of height gained. At the cruising height of most airliners, the outside temperature will be close to minus sixty degrees.

Clouds

Clouds can be found at most heights an airliner flies. However more will be present the lower you fly. They are classified according to the height they are likely to be found at and their appearance. There are a number of categories.

Low Clouds

There are three types to be found in this section and they are present up to a height of about 7,000 feet.

Stratus can be recognised as being usually dark grey in appearance and close to the ground. If these clouds are very close to the ground, the flight may have to be diverted to another airport.

Nimbostratus are clouds which are rain-bearing. Nimbus is a term which means rain-bearing. They can appear thick, dark and ragged at the edges. They can also be found covering the tops of mountains, so they can pose a hazard. However, this would only normally apply to much smaller aircraft flying visually. Modern airliners have a huge amount of equipment on board to help keep the aircraft away from such dangers.

Stratocumulus clouds appear as a layer of globular shapes which can be of a light or dark grey colour. From an aircraft's point of view, flying can become a bit bumpy due to the winds associated with them.

Medium Clouds

There are two types of medium cloud and they are usually found between heights of 7,000 feet and twenty thousand feet.

Altocumulus clouds appear as flattened globular shapes which are arranged in waves. Some people refer to these as a "mackerel sky."

Altostratus can appear as a layer of grey or bluish-grey cloud which is also fibrous.

High Clouds

High clouds have three types associated with them and they are classified as being found above twenty thousand feet. Because these clouds exist in a much cooler region of the atmosphere, they are likely to be composed of ice crystals rather than water droplets.

Cirrus

These are white in colour and appear as wispy without any particular shape to them.

Cirrocumulus clouds are also white in colour and take on the appearance of ripples across the sky.

Cirrostratus clouds appear as a thin white veil high in the sky. You may notice them as they can form a halo around the sun or moon.

Heaped Convection Clouds

There are two types of these clouds and can be found as low as one thousand feet to over thirty six thousand feet in height. More than any other, these clouds can affect an aircraft in flight, so weather radar and other measures are taken to minimise their effect.

Cumulus clouds are easily recognisable as the large, bright white cauliflower clouds that can fill a sky. They are often formed by hot air rising or by air being forced up due to high ground. Care should be taken as turbulent flying conditions may exist close to them.

Cumulonimbus clouds pose the biggest problem for aircraft as they are associated with thunderstorms and electrical activity. The air around them can be very turbulent and in extreme cases, be a threat to the aircraft. However, they show up on weather radar and are always reported by meteorology offices so avoiding action can be taken in plenty of time.

Fog

Fog can always pose a problem for aircraft taking off and landing. An aircraft will have a set of "minima" conditions which tell the pilot whether he or she is allowed to take off or land. Fog is caused when the air temperature reaches and then drops below its Dew Point which is the level where the air is said to be fully saturated. If the temperature drops further then the moisture held in the air condenses out in the form of fog. A light wind is also necessary to spread the fog into a larger mass.

Fuel Requirements

The cost of fuel today makes this the biggest factor when costing out a flight. On a short-haul flight, this would account for 75% of the complete cost. But on a long-haul flight, this percentage climbs to approximately 90% of the overall cost of the journey. So it is essential that every effort is made to keep this to a minimum.

The design of modern airliners has this factor near the top. In first place is of course safety. That is always the number one factor in flying. The new Boeing 787 Dreamliner is the latest aircraft to incorporate new design features into its construction which make it considerably more economic than its older rivals.

Deciding on the amount of fuel to carry is an important decision and one which finally rests with the captain of the flight. It is definitely not a case of just "filling her up" and off we go. Carrying additional fuel that will not be needed adds to the gross weight of the aircraft and therefore increases fuel consumption. It has been estimated that during a long-haul flight half of any additional fuel carried is used up just carrying that extra weight. So a fuel requirements calculation must be made.

In order to make the correct and safe calculation of the fuel requirement for a particular flight, a number of factors are taken into consideration. Any flight rarely goes exactly according to plan. There are just too many variables. For example, at busy airports your aircraft may have to queue up before taking off. It doesn't matter that you have a designated "slot time" to take off; if it is busy, you have to queue and that takes time and burns off more fuel.

So how does the pilot make his fuel calculation? Once again, the first factor to take into account is safety and aviation law lays down minimum fuel requirements for different stages of a flight. These include the following;-

Taxi fuel: this amount takes account of the distance involved and the time it is likely to take to get into the air. It also includes the taxi time at the destination airport.

Burn-Off Fuel: this is the amount of fuel that will be burnt off during the whole of the flight. It will include the fuel required to climb to the cruising altitude and descent into the destination airport.

Contingency Fuel: this is the estimation of the fuel required to cover any unforeseen problems or holdups. By law this is usually about 5% of the total burn-off fuel load. This is the extra that will be used if non-reported headwinds are met or diversion around thunderstorms etc. It also includes an amount necessary to reach the chosen alternate airport should the destination airport become unable to allow a landing. The alternate airport is named in the flight plan so the distances involved will be already known.

Reserve Fuel: this is extra fuel which is calculated to be needed if the aircraft is held in the hold. Many passengers arriving at busy airports or at busy times will have experienced the aircraft circling a fixed point awaiting permission to make its final approach and landing. These holding circuits normally last about four minutes each before descending to a lower altitude to fly another circuit. So the time can soon add up along with the extra fuel usage.

The captain will look carefully at these requirements for a particular flight and if there are no other factors which could increase the fuel used, he or she will sign off that amount to be uplifted into the aircraft before start-up. The final decision is that of the captain.

Weight and Balance

We earlier referred to the weight and balance of the aircraft when we mentioned the term load sheet. In essence what all this means is that before a flight can commence the pilot has to know the weight of the aircraft at various stages of the flight. The weight obviously diminishes during a flight as the fuel load is burnt off. But if the weight is too high or if it is loaded wrongly, the aircraft will be out of balance and may not be able to take-off under the current runway conditions.

All of these factors concern what we call the "performance" of an aircraft. The factors involved in working out the weight and balance do not include just the weight. Other factors such as wind, temperature, slope of the runway and condition of the runway surface all have an effect on performance and indicate to the pilot how much runway he needs to take-off and whether his weight on landing will not be too heavy.

The maximum landing weight is lower than the maximum take-off weight and therefore explains why we sometimes hear of a pilot "dumping fuel" before making an unscheduled landing. They are literally making the aircraft lighter in order to execute a safe landing.

So how is a load sheet calculated?

The first weight to take into account is that of the aircraft without any load or fuel on board. To this is added any special equipment. Next the weight of the crew and their personal luggage is added. The next stage is to add the weight of any cargo to be carried. Then the weight of the passenger luggage is calculated, followed by the combined weight of all the passengers. This total weight is known as the Zero Fuel Weight or ZFW.

All cargo must be loaded to ensure the aircraft remains in balance

In an earlier section we discussed how the correct amount of fuel for a particular flight is calculated. This fuel load expressed in tons is then added to the load sheet. This now gives the Take-Off Weight or TOW. This weight is checked to make sure that it is within the maximum weight allowable for the conditions.

But this is only half of the story. The weight of all the different loads put on the aircraft have to be positioned as to make sure that the aircraft's centre of gravity falls within the safe range expressed for the aircraft. The centre of gravity for an aircraft is said to act through a point along a line drawn from the leading edge of a wing to its trailing edge. In other words, it is a line drawn in cross-section from the front to the rear of the wing. This line is known as the Mean Aerodynamic Chord or MAC.

The centre of gravity point is expressed as a percentage along the line from the front of the wing. So, for example, if the centre of gravity is said to be 50%, it indicates that the centre of gravity is acting halfway along the wing. Each of the weights above will have a particular centre of gravity value. These are known as Zero Fuel Weight Centre of Gravity or ZFWCG and the Take-Off Weight Centre of Gravity or TOWCG. As an airline pilot you have to get used to dealing with a multitude of abbreviations.

There will be optimum percentages for an aircraft and the loadmaster will try to ensure that the final loading and centre of gravity will be as close to the recommended figures as possible. This figure will be checked by the captain and signed off before the flight. We already know that during a flight the weight of an aircraft changes. Therefore the crew have to plan to distribute the remaining fuel in order to keep the centre of gravity within safe limits.

One important point to note is that any last minute changes to the loading of an aircraft means that the load sheet must be altered and this can take time. For example, any luggage that does not tally with the manifest may have to be inspected and perhaps removed. This means recalculating the change and in some circumstances can lead to the flight being delayed. Also, if your hand luggage is found to be too big or heavy it may have to go in the hold and this can cause further delays.

"The theory I like best is that the Rings of Saturn are composed of lost airline luggage…"

Mark Russell

Chapter 3

Pre-Flight Preparation

Arrival at the Aircraft

Before the flight crew reach their aircraft they will have met in the Crew Briefing Office where the flight plan will have been checked again, the latest weather reports will have been checked and any further NOTAMS scrutinised. It may come as a surprise to some to hear that in large airline companies the captain and first officer (also known as the co-pilot) may not have met before meeting in the Crew Briefing Office.

This could alarm some passengers who might think that if they haven't met before how can they work together as a safe team? In extreme circumstances, if something were to go wrong, how would they know what the other one was thinking? The answer quite simply is that their training both as pilots and within their individual company ensures that everything, including emergencies will have been practised often and handled in ways that are laid out in regulations and manuals. The bottom line is that all crew members know exactly how to act as a team in almost every situation.

Pre-Flight Preparation

Before the crew bus takes them airside to the aircraft, the pilots and cabin crew will have had to go through security checks just like passengers. Their luggage will also have been checked. However, all members of the crew will carry security identification cards produced by their company which tell the security staff who they are. By the time they reach the aircraft there is probably less than one hour before departure.

The cabin crew may travel out to the aircraft on the same bus as the pilots but it is also possible that they may already be on board. If so, then the captain will introduce himself and then brief the chief cabin attendant as to the parts of the flight that will apply to their duties. This will include any expected weather problems that may delay the serving of meals etc. The chief flight attendant will then brief the rest of the cabin crew.

As with everything else in professional flying there are regulations that state how many cabin crew must be on duty for a particular aircraft. These regulations can vary depending on the aircraft. For example, the new Airbus A380 "Double-Decker" requires a minimum of eighteen flight attendants. This has been arrived at by requiring that there is one for each door on the aircraft plus an extra crew member for each floor.

At this stage, the cabin crew are busy ensuring that all meals, drinks and everything else that they require has been loaded aboard. They will also do a walk-through to ensure there are no suspicious articles where there should not be. Safety and security are once again at the top of the list of priorities.

The Walk-Round

Whether an aircraft is large or small, part of the pre-flight checks is a check of the outside of the plane. This inspection is either done by the captain or first officer. It is not necessarily true that this duty is carried out by the first officer if it is raining.

Whichever member of the aircrew is to make the inspection, they will first have to put on a high visibility vest or tabard. Before the pilot begins the inspection one of the ground engineers will also have made a full check of the exterior. However, a final inspection is always made by one of the pilots.

Some of the items he will be checking are whether any of the surfaces of the plane have been damaged. This could have happened recently by one of the ground operation trucks attending the aircraft. Though extremely unlikely, it is always best to be sure.

The pilot will also be looking to make sure that any covers have been removed from sensors such as the pitot tubes and that the undercarriage locking pins are removed. If everything checks out okay, he will climb aboard and re-join his colleague in the cockpit.

The Cockpit

Most modern airliners have what is called a "glass cockpit" and they have replaced the old "analogue" ones. These older style instrument panels were characterised by tens of individual glass instruments giving out information on just one or two functions. Most glass cockpits have replaced all of these with just eight TV style screens. Each of the screens has a multi-functional use and different displays can be called up by the pilot.

Glass cockpit of a modern airliner

TV style screens have replaced the old analogue instruments

If you look forward in such a cockpit you will see there are a matching set of two displays in front of each pilot. The screen on the left is known as the Primary Flight Display or PFD. The screen to the right of it is called the Navigational Display or ND. In the centre, between the two pilots is the Engine/Warning Display or EWD. Located in front of this screen and just forward of the thrust levers is the System Display or SD. Finally, to either side of the System Display is the Multi-Function Display or MFD. There is one of these for each pilot.

Let's take a closer look at them.

The pair of LCD screens in front of each pilot is known collectively as the Display Units or DUs. The Primary Flight Display on the left gives the pilot all the information about the flight characteristics of the aircraft. In the centre is the Attitude Indicator or AI which used to be known as the Artificial Horizon. This tells the pilot the orientation of the aircraft; whether it is in straight and level flight, whether it is climbing or descending or whether it is turning. A pilot could look out of the window to make these assessments but at night or in cloud, this isn't possible.

At the top of the Attitude Indicator is the Bank Angle Indicator which tells the pilot at what angle the aircraft is turning. Below the Attitude Indicator is the Heading Indicator which informs the pilot of their magnetic heading or the direction the aircraft is pointing.

To the left of the AI is the Airspeed Indicator and this reads the airspeed of the aircraft in nautical miles per hour. To the right of the AI is the Altimeter or Alt which measures the aircraft's altitude in feet and next to this is the Vertical Speed Indicator or VSI which gives the rate of change in height if the aircraft is ascending or descending.

At the very top of the screen is the Flight Mode Annunciator or FMA which can give the pilot a range of additional information such as the state of the autopilot.

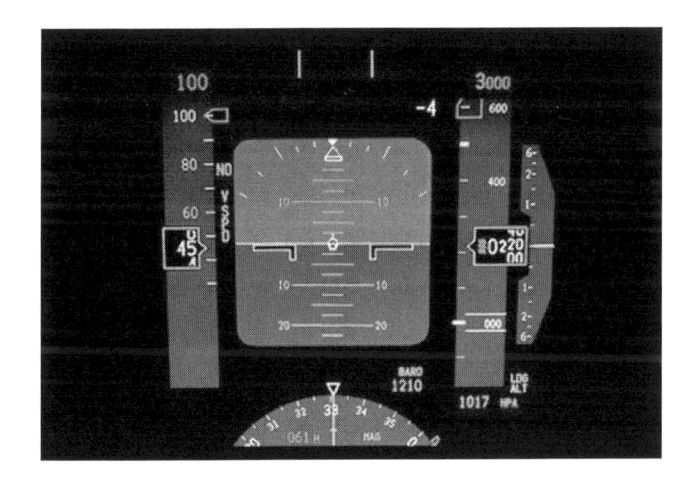

Primary Flight Display PFD

Next to the PFD is the Navigation Display (ND) which is the main display for information on the aircraft's route. A representation of the aircraft is shown in the centre of the screen. In front of it are painted semi-circular lines indicating distances. The final curved line indicates the magnetic heading of the aircraft.

When the flight plan has been entered into the computer, the ND will also display the planned route ahead. Other navigational beacons on the ground can also be selected by the pilot from the library stored within the computer memory banks.

Navigation Display ND

Another very useful function of the ND is that it can also display the weather that will be encountered ahead. The pilot will be able to see if there are clouds ahead and because they are colour coded, the captain will know if the predicted weather will cause any problems for the flight. The colours used are green, yellow and red; the latter is the more serious. What this means is that the pilot can if necessary, steer the aircraft around any bad weather that may be up ahead. The latest aircraft even show a vertical representation of the weather ahead. This tells the pilot whether he can fly above or below the problem rather than fly around it.

On the centre console between both pairs of DUs is the Engine/Warning Display (EWD). The screen can be split into two areas. The upper part of the screen displays the information the pilot needs to know about the functioning of each engine. The lower area will immediately show any problem or malfunction of an engine system.

This is perhaps a good time just to mention how an engine failure affects the aircraft from the point of view of a passenger. The answer is hardly at all. Most short to medium range airliners will have two jet engines. Long-haul aircraft such as the Boeing 747, Airbus 340 and Airbus 380 will have four engines. If there is any reason for the pilot of an aircraft with two engines to have to shut one down, the power contained within the remaining engine is so great that the aircraft will continue to fly without any problem. We will discuss the jet engine in more detail in the next chapter.

Top: Navigation Displays and Engine Warning Display in centre

Below: Multi-Function Displays and Systems Display in centre

Below the EWD there is another screen which is termed the Systems Display (SD). As its name implies, it presents to the pilots information on the various aircraft systems during a flight. Because there are so many different systems aboard the plane, the captain can call up any system he wishes by keying in a few commands. The keyboard for this is called the ECAM Control Panel or ECP where ECAM stands for Electronic Centralised Aircraft Monitoring. It is located behind the thrust levers.

Some of the schematic displays which can be called up include pressurisation, air conditioning, hydraulic systems, tyre pressures, flight control surfaces, fuel control, additional engine readouts, security of doors and hatches and electrical systems.

On either side of the Systems Display screen there is a Multi-Function Display (MFD); one for each pilot. Together with their individual keyboards, each pilot is able to access the Flight Management Computer or FMC and the other computers which are installed aboard the aircraft. All sorts of data can be called up in seconds.

Multi-Function Displays MFD – one for each pilot

The throttles are in the centre

To the general passenger this may all sound rather complicated but the design of these modern cockpits makes the vital information an aircrew needs during a flight very readily and easily accessible.

They have a logical approach and using them becomes quite straightforward.

There are a number of other individual controls and instruments worth mentioning. One is the Mach Meter. This measures the aircraft's airspeed. But wait, we have already said we have an airspeed indicator ASI as part of the Primary Flight Display. However, because the density of air reduces with height, measuring airspeed above 25,000 feet becomes a little difficult for the ASI. Therefore we use a Mach Meter which measures the ratio of the True Airspeed TAS to the speed of sound at that particular height.

The speed of sound also reduces as height is gained. This is because the temperature drops as we fly higher. The difference is quite large. At sea-level, the speed of sound is about 660 knots but at 30,000 feet, it has reduced to approximately 590 knots. On a Mach Meter the speed of sound is 1.0 so speeds will be a fraction of this number. For example, an aircraft may cruise at Mach 0.55. Concorde of course was one of the exceptions where its Mach Meter would read in excess of 2.0 at cruising level.

We will be mentioning the autopilot from time to time in this book. Most people overestimate its ability. An autopilot does not think for itself. The pilot does not press a button and the autopilot just flies the plane automatically to the destination. It can do this, but it must first be programmed to fly a particular route by the aircrew. It won't do anything unless the pilots have keyed in the correct instructions. Having said this, a properly programmed autopilot can fly to a very, very high order of accuracy and it does not suffer from tiredness.

It may surprise you to learn that the first simple autopilot system was first demonstrated as far back as 1914. These days a modern airliner will have a number of autopilot systems in place, so that if one should malfunction, another can take its place. On some aircraft there is even an autoland system which allows the complete landing and braking to take place without the pilots manually operating the aircraft. But to facilitate this, the airport also has to have very sophisticated ground equipment available. Suffice it to say, that it is likely that your landing will be handled by a human pilot and not a computer.

There are a number of other panels and controls in the cockpit of a modern airliner and we will cover these as we progress through our flight. But we will finish this section by mentioning the control column which many years ago was also referred to as the "joystick". Many passengers will think of it as a type of steering wheel standing on a pedestal in front of each pilot. This is still the case in many aircraft.

However, the latest airliners have a much smaller control situated to the side of them. It looks very similar to the joystick found with many home computers. Operation of it is the same as the older style wheel; pull it back and the aircraft climbs, push it forward and the aircraft descends. By moving it to the left or right, the aircraft will bank in that direction. So the next time you are flying your computer flight simulation programme, your control will not be that dissimilar to the real thing.

Ground Operations

Whilst the aircrew are conducting some of their pre-flight preparations, the passengers will have been processed. Their luggage will have been taken at the check-in desk. Next their identities will be confirmed at passport control. Finally a security check of each person and their hand luggage will be made before they are called to the Departure Lounge ready for boarding.

During this same time, on the apron around the aircraft it is a hive of activity. A variety of services will be loading the aircraft with the supplies it needs for the flight. We have already mentioned that the correct fuel amount must be uplifted and signed off by the captain. The type of fuel used in airliners is called kerosene and is titled Jet A1. We will discuss the characteristics of using kerosene in the section on the jet engine.

Fuel being uploaded into the port wing tank

Fuel is uplifted into the aircraft's fuel tanks via a fuel bowser. The fuel tanks are located in each wing. On some larger aircraft there is also an additional fuel tank in the belly of the plane. Because a great deal of fuel needs to be loaded, the bowser can deliver it at a rate of up to 3,000 litres a minute. The fuel pipes are connected to valves on the lower side of each wing. The process is mostly automatic; the ground engineer keys in the amount of fuel to be uploaded and then presses the "auto-start" button and off it goes.

The luggage that has been checked in will now be loaded into the hold and any additional cargo also loaded in a way that maintains the aircraft's centre of gravity within the safe range. The final load sheet will be signed off by the captain. Food and drinks for the flight will also have been loaded and checked by the cabin crew.

Various services preparing an airliner for flight

A truck will fill up the drinking water tanks whilst another truck called the "honey wagon" removes toilet waste and replaces it with new clean water. So the old urban legend that toilet waste is dumped out into the air after flushing the toilet is definitely not true.

"In the space age, man will be able to

go around the world in two hours –

One hour for flying and one hour to get to the airport…"

Neil McElroy, "Look" 1958

Chapter 4

Start-Up and Taxi

The Jet Engine

The jet engine was a British invention by Sir Frank Whittle in 1937 but the first jet aircraft was a single seat German plane, the Heinkel 178. Britain took the lead again with the world's first jet airliner. This was the Comet 4. However, regular jet transatlantic travel did not begin until nine years later in 1958. Since then, jet travel has increased enormously. Since it is the means of getting an aircraft into the sky, let's take a closer look on how such an engine works.

In essence a modern jet engine is quite a simple design. If you look at the front of one you will see lots of blades splaying outwards from a central hub. This is why this type of engine is known as a fan jet. Walk to the side and you will also notice that the engine tapers off slightly along its length and ends in an exhaust at the aft end.

Basically what happens is that air is taken in via the fan blades at the front. This air is then compressed via a compressor. It then enters the combustion chamber where it is mixed with burning fuel. This causes the gas mixture to expand enormously and very quickly. The gases now power a turbine which in turn helps to drive the compressor. The gases are then exhausted out at very great speed. The reaction to these gases being vented backwards is to propel the aircraft forward. This is a good example of Newton's Third Law of Motion in action; "to every action there is an equal and opposite reaction."

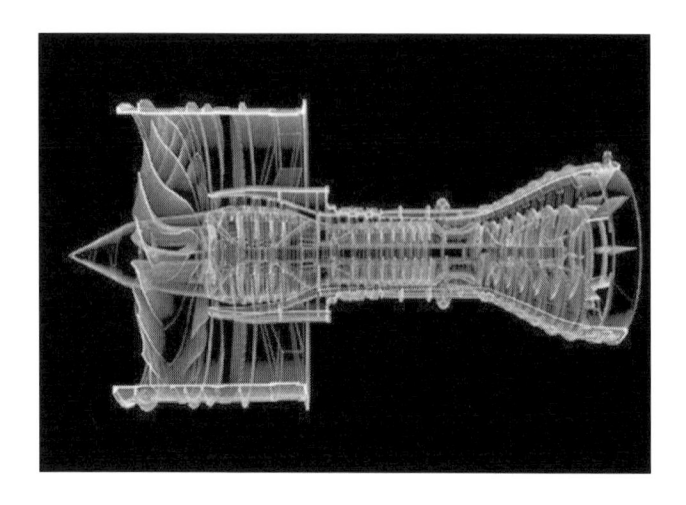

Schematic of a modern jet engine

The type of jet aircraft you will fly on will probably have engines which are more advanced than this simple example. They may be called bypass engines which means that up to five times the air that is taken into the engine bypasses the compressors and combustion system and instead is vented directly to the exhaust pipe. Up to 75% of the engine thrust may be created this way.

A modern jet engine will also have more than one compressor. Many will have three and they are each termed by the letter "N". From the front the first compressor after the air is taken in by the fan blades is known as the N1 spool. It is a low pressure compressor. Further along the engine are the N2 and N3 spools and these are high pressure compressors. Earlier it was mentioned that the fuel used is kerosene. This has a quality which is very important to this type of engine. It does not ignite immediately but instead, burns continuously.

Fan blades draw air into the N 1 compressor

It should go without saying that you should never stand in the front or directly behind one of these engines unless it is completely shut-down. To give you an idea of the power these engines command, even if the engine is only idling, a person can be sucked into the fan blades if they stand within ten metres of the front. At the rear of the engine behind the exhaust outlet, a person can be knocked over at a distance of fifty metres.

Pre-Flight Systems Checks

The passengers will now be boarding the aircraft and both pilots will be in the cockpit going through all of the pre-flight checklists. The ground engineer who has also made a separate check as to the serviceability of the aircraft presents his documentation to the captain for him to sign off. Any problems that may have been found must be attended to before the aircraft is cleared to fly.

However, it is possible for an aircraft to have one or two minor problems. If this is the case, the engineer and captain will consult the aircraft's Minimum Equipment List or MEL which lays out the minimum that is required of each aircraft system. Because a modern airliner has so many back-up systems, a small fault in one may be allowable. If this is so, a note is made in the aircraft's Deferred Defect Log. This means that the defect will be attended to as soon as time allows. This may be when the aircraft reaches its "base" airport. But remember, these faults are small and are safely supported by other back-up systems, so there will not be any danger to the flight.

At the same time all the paperwork and documentation pertaining to the plane are checked to make sure they are all current. These will include the Certificate of Airworthiness and the Certificate of Maintenance. All aircraft have to undergo minor and major servicing after so many hours in the air. These are laid down in law and must be adhered to and then a certificate produced to verify this. The flying licenses of the crew are also checked to make sure their medical certificates and flying hours are in order.

Crews work through exhaustive checklists before a flight

As the crew work their way through the checklists, we can take a look at some of the aircraft systems that they will be checking.

Pressurisation and Air Conditioning

Most people know that the cabin of an airliner when flying is pressurised. At the normal cruising altitudes of around 35,000 feet, the outside air pressure is so low as to be of immediate danger to life. In addition, the outside air temperature will be around -60 degrees Celsius. Therefore the cabin needs to be pressurised to a comfortable altitude and the air conditioning set to deliver a normal temperature.

When the aircraft is on the ground, the air conditioning is supplied with compressed air which is derived from the Auxiliary Power Unit or APU. We will talk more about the APU later in this chapter. When in-flight, the air for the air conditioning is bled off from the engines and not from the atmosphere outside. Coming from the engines this air will be hot so it is cooled through heat exchangers called Air Cooling Machines or ACMs.

The amount of "new" air is reduced by recirculating a proportion of the cabin air. This has the result of using less fuel. The cargo holds also use air from the cabin and at least one of the holds will be able to be heated. This is in case the aircraft is carrying live animals etc.

The other use of the air conditioning system is to pressurise the aircraft. As we have said before, when the aircraft is at cruise level, the air pressure outside is too low to support life. Therefore the interior of the aircraft has to be pressurised to a positive value compared with outside. It works on the principle that if the air drawn into the aircraft is greater than the air leaving it, then the pressure within must be positive.

It may be assumed that this interior pressure is the same as would be experienced on the ground at sea-level. This assumption is wrong. If this were the case, the aircraft would have to be strengthened to cope with the greater pressure difference. This in turn would make the aircraft heavier and therefore less efficient.

Instead, the cabin pressure is set at about 6-7,000 feet. This means that it is equivalent to a person breathing air at a height of approximately 6,000 feet. This altitude is more than comfortable for passengers and crew. To maintain the pressure, there are a number of outflow valves which regulate the airflow. The humidity aboard an aircraft tends towards the dry side. So it is always a good idea to drink plenty of fluids and by this, we mean water.

The pressurisation of the aircraft is gradual and automatic. When the aircraft takes off the computer begins to pressurise the cabin. As it climbs and gains height, the pressure in the cabin also changes but at a slower rate so that by the time the plane reaches its cruising altitude, let's say 37,000 feet, the cabin pressure will have reached 6,000 feet. If in the rare case of the system failing, the pilot can take over manually and select different altitude pressure levels.

At this point, let's answer a question asked by many passengers. "Is it possible to open the door when the aircraft is cruising?" The answer is "no." This is so even though the door is unlocked. However, to open a door it must be first pulled in towards you before it opens out. And if you think about it, the pressure difference means that the door is being pushed outwards against the frame. From about 10,000 feet upwards the force required to open the door is way beyond what a person could ever accomplish. So there is no chance of a person opening one of the doors when the aircraft is at height.

Fuel Management Systems

We have already talked a little about fuel. However there is a lot more to managing the fuel during a flight than just "filling her up" and off we go. The fuel load has to be distributed around the aircraft in different ways depending on the stage of the flight. It has already been mentioned that most of the fuel is carried in tanks located in the aircraft's wings. The weight of the fuel will obviously have an effect on the structure of the aircraft.

Therefore, when the plane is on the ground, the fuel is distributed in the tanks closer to the fuselage. This has the effect of taking the strain off the ends of the wings and concentrating it where the wings are wider and stronger. If you think about it, this action stops the wings from bending downwards with the weight.

However, when the aircraft takes off, there will now be a tendency for the wings to bend upwards as lift takes over. Therefore the fuel is distributed more equally along the entire wing to compensate for this effect. The entire operation can be automatic via the Fuel Quantity Management System or FQMS. At each stage of the flight it will distribute the remaining fuel so as to maintain the aircraft's balance and centre of gravity.

The fuel tanks themselves have differing functions. Some are termed feeder tanks which means they feed the engines to keep them running. These tanks are continually supplied by storage tanks so that the flow of fuel to the engines is maintained throughout. To enable all this to happen, there are a number of fuel pumps. There are also booster pumps and collector tanks which come into play when the aircraft's attitude changes; for example, at take-off. What all this means is that no matter what configuration the aircraft is in, there will always be fuel being fed to the engines.

At this point, let's consider the very unlikely event of an aircraft needing to land earlier than planned. It was said earlier that the landing weight is lower than the take-off weight. Landing "heavy" is safe but can overstress the aircraft. To alleviate this problem, the aircraft can be made lighter by jettisoning fuel. All the pilot has to do is tell the computer what the desired landing weight is and then press the fuel jettison button. The computer will then select and distribute the fuel by dumping the extra through small jettison nozzles on the trailing edge of the wing. The aircraft can then carry out a normal landing at the correct weight.

On-Board Electrical Systems

The electrical systems during a flight are supplied by generators powered by each of the engines. The power produced is alternating current at 115 volts. This in turn can be converted via rectifiers to direct current which is used to power the equipment on board. The electrical system on an aircraft is separated into "essential" and "emergency". This means that priority is given to all systems which are important to the safety of a flight.

However, even if all the generators aboard the aircraft were to fail, power can still be generated. There are back-up batteries for each engine generator. In addition, the Auxiliary Power Unit (APU) can also be started up. This is the unit which generates power to the aircraft when it is on the ground. You can see its exhaust nozzle at the very rear of the fuselage just below the tail.

In addition to all this the pilot can also use the RAT. This is the Ram Air Turbine and is a propeller device which drops below the aircraft and into the airflow. This causes the propeller to turn and generate power. The amount of power it can produce is about 10% of normal. But this is enough to power all the essential equipment the aircraft needs to fly safely.

Fire Protection Systems

One of the biggest fears most people may have is the prospect of fire on board when the aircraft is in the air and one of the commonest scenarios is an engine fire. Once again, such things are extremely rare but if ever it should occur there are systems in place to handle it.

There are basically two types of detection systems employed on board. The first are called fire detection loops and they are located within the engine cowlings. The second type is smoke detectors and these can be found in electrical equipment bays, cargo holds and the toilets. These are places where the crew cannot be expected to be able to observe throughout a flight.

If we first take the scenario of an engine fire, we can see how the pilots deal with it safely. At the first sign of fire within an engine, the pilots are alerted by visual and audio alarms in the cockpit. There is a fire control panel and various indicators will light to inform the pilot what it is and where the problem is located. The operation is termed an "isolate and extinguish" sequence.

First the pilot will shut-down the engine which is shown to have the fire problem. This is a simple operation of pulling back the throttle control to that engine and then switching off that engine's master switch. The pilot will then look at the fire control panel. A large red button will be illuminated. This will have the words "Fire-Push" printed on it. The pilot will do what it says "on the label" and depress it.

The effect of this action is to cut-off the fuel supply to the engine in question and to isolate any services such as electrics and hydraulics to it. It also has the effect of arming the fire extinguisher system. There are two such extinguisher systems for each engine and they are termed "Agent 1" and "Agent 2". The button controlling Agent 1 is pressed and the fire extinguisher bottle located within the engine compartment is activated. The pilot will now wait for about thirty seconds to confirm that the fire has been extinguished. If this is not the case the second fire extinguishing bottle will be activated by pressing the button marked Agent 2.

If there is a fire in one of the cargo holds, then the pilot will first cut-off the air to the hold and then activate the fire extinguisher bottles. The first will activate immediately and the second bottle will follow. But the second one will activate over a longer period of time to allow the maximum time for the smothering effects to work. It also gives the crew plenty of time to divert to an alternative airport if required.

Each toilet will have both a fire and smoke detector. If a fire is detected, a fire extinguisher will automatically activate in the waste area. The smoke detector will also send a warning both to the cockpit and cabin crew. Any further fire can then be tackled by the crew with hand-held fire extinguishers. So never light a cigarette on board as you will be detected.

Other Systems

As the crew move through all the pre-flight checklists they will be uploading the route into the navigation system. We will take a closer look at how a plane is navigated in the chapter about cruising. The crew will also be checking the autopilot system. This will be used during a large part of the flight, so checks are made to ensure it is set up correctly.

When all the pre-flight work has been completed, it is time to start the engines before taxiing out to the active runway.

Engine Start and Push-Back

Just before we start the engines ready for departure, let's spend a little time describing the general duties of the flight crew and how they go about their work behind the locked door of the cockpit.

On most airliners there will be two pilots; the captain and the first officer. Long-haul flights will often carry an extra pilot so that a crew member can be rested during a long flight. Many passengers believe that it is always the captain who flies the plane and the co-pilot is there to assist. This is not correct. What happens in real life is that the actual operation of flying the aircraft is shared. For example, the captain may fly the aircraft out to the destination and the first officer will fly the plane back.

Captain and First Officer take turns to fly the aircraft

These responsibilities are termed Pilot Flying (PF) and Pilot Non-Flying (PNF). If you think about it, this makes sense. If the first officer never flew the aircraft how could they gain the experience to achieve their own command in the future? Remember, the first officer is already a well-trained and highly qualified pilot. If they weren't, they wouldn't be sitting in the cockpit in the first place.

So how are the duties separated out between the two pilots? The Pilot Flying is responsible for all the flight control of the aircraft; they fly the plane and also give orders for different controls to be selected. The Pilot Non-Flying is responsible for carrying out these orders. They also make all of the radio calls and keep the paperwork up to date as the flight progresses.

On our flight, we will assume that the captain has elected to be the Pilot Flying and the first officer as PNF. This means that the Flight Briefing will be carried out by the captain. A flight briefing does what it sounds like; it covers the final paperwork and plan of departure from the airport. This means that any NOTAMS are checked for the departure airport. The captain will also discuss which taxiway will be used to reach the active runway. One of the important parts of the briefing will always cover what they will do if a problem should arise at any point during the departure process.

For example, they will already be aware at what speed the aircraft will take-off at or "rotate" off the runway. But there will also be a speed at which if a problem should arise and the plane has not taken off, the crew will still fly the aircraft off the runway. This speed is known as V1 and means that it is the speed where there is not enough room left on the runway to stop safely. For instance, there could be a very rare engine failure at or slightly above V1. Even on one engine, the aircraft can safely take-off and climb before returning and making a safe landing. All of these rare eventualities are discussed and a plan of action agreed upon. Most of these are standard procedures already laid down by the aviation authorities.

ATC must first give permission before Start-Up

When this briefing is complete, a radio call may be made to ATC in order to obtain a clearance for their departure route. On some aircraft this can be done via a data link and the clearance will be returned as a printed message. The departure route clearance will include such topics as the active runway in use, the transponder code to be transmitted (this allows the air traffic controllers to identify and track a particular aircraft), the Standard Instrument Departure or SID (this is the cleared route from the departure airport) and finally and most importantly, the aircraft's slot time. This is the time at which the aircraft has been given in order to take-off. If it is missed, it may mean a lengthy wait. This will be given as "Zulu" time or Greenwich Mean Time or UTC; these are all different terms for the same time standard.

Now comes another checklist; the Before Start checklist. Once this has been completed, it is time for the aircraft to be pushed back. Once this has happened, the engines can be started. The first officer calls the "Ground" part of the ATC unit and requests "push back." When this is granted, he will use the intercom to relay the clearance message to the ground engineer who drives the push back truck. Anti-collision beacons are switched on to warn all personnel on the ground that the engines are about to start.

As the truck pushes the aircraft away from the terminal the passengers may hear the usual message over the intercom, "Cabin crew, set doors to automatic." This means that the doors are now armed and ready to automatically deploy chutes which can be used if the aircraft should need to be evacuated. After landing, the order, "Doors to manual" may also be heard.

Engine Start Panel

The engines will be started in order. Sitting aboard the aircraft, number 1 engine is on the far left of you, number 2 on the left inboard, number 3 inboard on the right and number 4 outboard on the right. This obviously applies to a four engine aircraft. One point to note is that the engines are usually started right to left, so number 2 is likely to be started before number 1.

Starting a jet engine is fairly straightforward from the crew's point of view. The captain will select the Engine Start switch and rotate it to the Ignition Start position. At this point, passengers may notice that the air conditioning in the cabin drops off. This is because all of the compressed air being generated through the aircraft's Auxiliary Power Unit (APU) is needed to turn the high pressure compressor in the engine.

Next the fuel master switch to that particular engine is turned on. The air flows into the combustion chamber and the fuel is introduced and mixed with it. Then the igniters operate and the hot gases are then vented from the rear exhaust pipes. This in turn helps to power the engine turbines until they become self-sustaining. Once they reach this point, the starter motor turns itself off.

Aircraft being "pushed back"

Engine start-up is about to begin

The same sequence is carried out for the other engine. For this example we will consider our aircraft to have two engines and not three or four. The engines will stabilise themselves when they reach "idle" power. If there is a problem when starting, the fuel will be automatically cut-off and the fan blades will continue to turn in order to cool the engine. A second attempt will then be made. If there is a second failure, the system will be shut-down and engineers will be called.

The aircraft has now been pushed back and permission has been given for the engineer to disconnect the truck. Both engines are at idle power. The After Start checklist can now be actioned. This will consist of turning the APU off as the engines are now supplying all power.

Take-off flap configuration will be selected. These can be seen as panels drooping from the trailing edge of the wings. There are also flaps on the leading edge and these are called Kruger flaps. Their main job is to provide additional lift at take-off and allow a slower approach speed at landing. It is now time to begin taxiing the aircraft out to the active runway.

Taxi to the Runway

The first action that must be taken by the crew is to request permission to taxi. At large airports it can get very busy and the controllers in charge of ground movements need to know the intentions of every aircraft crew. Once permission is granted, the throttles can be moved forward and the brakes released. The aircraft slowly begins to taxi.

Just as with driving down a road there are speed and other regulations set in place in order to keep all aircraft separated. The route to the holding point of the runway will be known to the crew and will have been confirmed in the clearance. This is also the time to test a few other systems. For example, each pilot will have tested his brakes. These are activated by pressing the tops of the rudder pedals. It is important to note that these are not the main braking system used upon landing but we will discuss this subject in a later chapter.

The aircraft can be steered on the ground by using the rudder pedals. However, if a larger or tighter turn is required, there is a small control near the control column that turns the nose-wheel. Speed must be carefully controlled when turning a large aircraft on the ground as there can be a tendency for the nose-wheel to skid.

During this time the chief member of the cabin crew will indicate via the Flight Attendant Panel or FAP to the captain that the passenger cabin is ready for departure. The Before Take-Off checklist is also completed except for a couple of items. There can often be a short queue of aircraft awaiting permission to take-off. Our crew will wait at the holding point until called forward to line-up.

Maximum speeds and rules apply when taxiing

All ATC instructions must be read-back by the Pilot Non-Flying so that the controller knows that the crew have heard the instructions correctly. If a crew misheard an instruction to hold and instead taxied out onto the runway just as another aircraft was landing, then the consequences could be very serious. Therefore, all instructions are repeated.

When the permission to line-up is heard and confirmed, the captain calls for the "Below the Line" checks and this means that the

PNF finishes the checklist off. As the aircraft taxies out onto the runway, it must be remembered that permission to line-up is not a permission to take-off. Another aircraft may have already been granted permission to cross the active runway so it would be very dangerous to start the take-off run before permission was given. When the aircraft is on the centre line of the runway, the crew wait for permission to take-off.

The captain will alert the cabin crew that the take-off roll is about to commence by switching the seat belt signs off and then on again. All is ready and the crew await the permission to take-off call.

Passenger: "Is this old aeroplane safe to fly?

Pilot: Just how in the world do you think it got this old...?

Anon

Chapter 5

Take-Off and Climb

Take-Off Run

The permission to take-off call is received and confirmed back to the controller. The captain acting as the Pilot Flying has checked if there is any crosswind which may affect the take-off. If there is and it is below the safety value, he will compensate using the primary flight controls.

The captain now advances the throttles to about 30% of maximum thrust with the brakes still applied. A few seconds are taken to allow the engines to stabilise and to ensure that there are no problems. Then he advances the throttles forwards again and releases the brakes. The aircraft begins to accelerate and the passengers feel that gentle force pushing them back into their seats. Although some people do not like this initial sensation, I personally feel it is one of the most exciting experiences in the world.

The throttles are now set at Flexible/Maximum Continuous Thrust or FLX MCT which sets the power to a value which was input earlier. This could be in the region of 90% of maximum power. If for any reason full power is required, the captain can push the throttle levers forwards to the Take-Off/Go-Around setting. This is shown as TOGA on the thrust console.

The aircraft is now gaining speed quickly; the captain holding the centre line of the runway using the rudder pedals. The first officer checks that the thrust setting is correct and calls "Thrust Set" to confirm this. At about 80 knots, the airspeed indicators are cross-checked to ensure they are in agreement. If they are not, the take-off is aborted. But they agree and the run continues.

Speed V1 – Rotate – Take-Off

When the speed which is V1 for this take-off is reached, the captain will take his right hand off the throttle levers because the aircraft is now committed to taking to the air. The crew are now looking for the next critical speed. This is known as Vr and is the speed at which the aircraft can rotate and begin to leave the runway. The pilot now pulls gently back on the control column and the nose of the aircraft lifts. He continues this action to a pre-planned angle; by the time it reaches this it will have left the runway and be starting its climb out.

The crew are now looking to reach V2 which is the take-off safety speed. The climb speed is set to V2 + 10 knots and the aircraft continues to gain height. The captain now calls for the undercarriage to be raised with the order, "Gear Up." The first officer pulls up the undercarriage lever and the three green lights near it turn to red. This indicates that the landing gear is in transit. They will go out when the undercarriage is safely stored and the hatches closed.

Climb to Cruising Level

It is quite common for the pilot to manually fly the aircraft in the initial stages of a climb before selecting the autopilot. However, at some major airports there are strict noise abatement procedures in force. This means that departing aircraft have to keep to very tight routes. Failure to keep to these routes by only a small distance may result in a very heavy fine. Therefore in such cases the crew will switch the autopilot on earlier. It is a sobering fact that the computers controlling the autopilot are more accurate than a human pilot. In this example, we will assume that the aircraft is hand-flown to a height of 10,000 feet before the autopilot is engaged.

As the aircraft gains height the throttle levers are pulled back slightly to the CL mark on the throttle base. This stands for climb power and it also can bring the auto-thrust programme into action. The power will now be set automatically to optimum until the aircraft levels out at its initial cruise height. At about 4,000 feet the take-off flaps will be retracted. They are usually brought up in stages and at specific speeds. The captain will order the final stage of flap to be retracted with the words, "Flaps zero." When the first officer sees that the flaps are fully retracted he confirms it with the reply, "Flaps are zero." The After Take-Off checklist is then displayed and the items are ticked off by the Pilot Non-Flying.

As height is gained the aircraft will approach what is termed the transition altitude. This altitude will vary from place to place but what it means is that the altimeter has to be reset to a standard pressure setting. This is 1013 millibars or HectoPascals as these units are now called. In the USA, inches of mercury are used as the standard unit of measuring pressure. All aircraft above the transition altitude will be using the same standard pressure setting. Therefore the altitude shown in each cockpit will be the same which makes vertical separation of aircraft more accurate and therefore safer.

Below the transition altitude, two settings are used and these are termed QNH and QFE. These will vary with changing air pressure so ATC will update these values and transmit them to aircraft before take-off and on approach to land. The QNH is the height of an aircraft above sea-level whilst the QFE is the height above a particular piece of the ground. This is often the highest point of the active runway in use but it can vary.

During the climb the crew will also be asked to change frequency so that another branch of Air Traffic Control can guide them further on their journey. The crew will also be requested to "Squawk Ident." If you recall, we mentioned transponder codes earlier and said that it was a way for ATC to positively identify particular aircraft. By pressing the Ident button the four number code which was given to the crew will now be displayed and highlighted on the radar screen of the controller. The controller will now know exactly where our aircraft is located and its altitude.

This is a good time to mention that there are also specific four digit codes which alert ground controllers as to the condition of the aircraft without the need of the pilot to radio in the information. For example, a code showing 7500 indicates that there is some interference to the flight. In a worst case scenario, this could indicate a terrorist incident or attempted high-jacking. A code of 7600 indicates that there is a problem with the radio and the crew cannot transmit any verbal information. Finally, there is 7700 which indicates that there is an emergency on board. These three codes are not often used but they are always available if the unlikely need ever arises.

Climbing to Cruise Altitude

At different points along the climb, ATC will clear the aircraft to the next level. As the assigned cruise level is approached the captain will call out, "One to go." This indicates that there is 1,000 feet before the cruise level is reached. The autopilot will now adjust the power setting from CLM to ALT CRZ which will be the most efficient cruising speed for the aircraft. It will also level the plane out. This point in the flight is called "Top of Climb." In our particular flight we will assume our cruising level is 36,000 feet or Flight Level 360 (FL 360).

"There are only two things required to fly a modern airliner – a pilot and a dog. It's the pilot's job to feed the dog. It's the dog's job to bite the pilot if he touches anything in the cockpit…"

Anon

Chapter 6

On-Route Flight

Passenger Services

For this section let's leave the captain and first officer in the cockpit and describe some of the things that passengers may encounter in the main cabin during the flight. Some of these will have safety implications and others may just give you an insight which may make your average flight more enjoyable.

If the weather is calm the Seatbelt signs will have already been turned off. When passengers see this, many of them immediately undo their belts completely, even if they plan to stay sitting in their seats. This is not a great idea. It is much more sensible to keep your seatbelt loosely fastened as any sudden turbulence will not cause any undue problems. It is rare for aircraft to encounter serious turbulence that has not been predicted but it does happen now and again. Certain phenomena such as wind-shear may not become apparent on the weather radar. These are known as CATs or Clear Air Turbulence. So if the seatbelt sign comes on again, you do not have to fiddle around looking for it.

One of the subjects you may have heard about in recent years is the possibility of getting Deep Vein Thrombosis or DVT whilst on board. This can occur in very rare circumstances and the person concerned is likely to already have a condition which makes this more likely. It can be caused by staying in your seat for hours on end. This is a much more likely scenario on long-haul flights rather than short-haul ones. There are a number of recommended actions in order to prevent DVT. Special socks are available and there are a range of exercises one can do whilst remaining in your seat. These can all help. However, my personal technique is to get up every two hours or so and have a walk around for five minutes to stretch the legs and get the circulation going.

Throughout this book I have emphasised the safety of flying as a form of travel and this is absolutely correct. However, in very rare circumstances a problem can occur which needs action to be taken by individual passengers. This is why it is always good sense to pay attention to the safety briefing at the beginning of each flight. And it doesn't matter if you are a regular flyer, you may be on an aircraft of a different type which may have exits in a different part of the aircraft and you need to check which exit is closest to your seat.

Another part of the safety briefing involves what to do if there is a pressurisation problem during the flight. Most passengers know that in such circumstances facemasks automatically drop from the ceiling in front of each passenger. The action required by each person is to tug on it; this releases the oxygen supply to the mask and you then put the mask over your nose and mouth and breathe normally. This sounds very simple when you hear it being briefed on the ground.

But it has been noted that approximately half of all passengers that have been required to do this for real haven't managed it. This may be due to surprise and a bit of panic. It may also be due to the fact that a sudden depressurisation can cause the atmosphere within the cabin to temporarily become very misty. This may confuse some passengers.

Remember also, two very important things. The mask is only centimetres from you so reach out, pull the chord and put it on. The mist will soon clear. And the other point to note is that a sudden depressurisation is often practised by the crew and they are trained to deal with it safely. It is very rare but if it happens, there is no need to panic.

On the lighter side of having a pleasurable flight, did you know that coffee tastes better than tea when flying? The reason for this lies in the cabin pressurisation of the aircraft. Because the cabin is pressurised to about a height of 6,000 feet, it means that water does not boil at 100 degrees Celsius as it does on the ground. On board it will boil at about 90 degrees.

This means that the boiling water is slightly cooler and as everyone knows, tea tastes better if it is boiling at 100 degrees. Coffee seems to have more latitude and tastes fine at 90 degrees. If we take this to extremes, making a cup of tea at the top of Mount Everest would be pretty difficult as the water boils at a very low temperature.

Okay, it is now time to join the aircrew in the cockpit again and look at two of the subjects which will be occupying them for the cruise duration of the flight; navigation and communication.

Navigation

If you have ever seen old aviation movies where the pilot is homing in to a beacon in order to find his way or a navigator in the rear of the cockpit bent over an air chart using dead reckoning to find the next waypoint, then let me assure you, those days are long gone. They were replaced decades ago by systems that use on-board gyros to calculate the position of the aircraft. However, all pilots during their training have to learn to use charts and plot their position in the air.

The present system uses laser guided gyros and is termed the Inertial Reference System or IRS. It is used in conjunction with a Global Positioning Satellite System (GPSS). The system uses the same technology and principle behind the type of GPS system found in motor vehicles, only it is a lot more accurate. In fact the separation between aircraft has been reduced by using this method. It can even allow some approaches to be made down to a very low level without using any beacons or equipment on the ground.

The system is not static; new satellites are being added by other countries so that the service will improve and accuracy further enhanced. This can lead to fully automatic landings in the future by most aircraft.

If we now join our aircrew that have the aircraft in the cruise at an altitude of 36,000 feet, we can look at the navigation system being used. Before the plane took off the pilots would have entered the route into the on-board Flight Management Computer (FMC). This can be accomplished via a data link or entered manually through the keyboards of the Multi-Function Displays. The FMC has a database on its hard drive so it is possible to enter some basic information and a choice of acceptable routings will be displayed. This database is updated on a regular basis and can cut down programming time.

Global Positioning Satellites and Inertial Reference Systems

are used for navigation

If you remember that when we discussed the cockpit layout in a previous section, it was stated that there is a Navigational Display (ND) in front of each pilot and to the right of the Primary Flight Display (PFD). It can be configured in a number of ways but its main screen shows the route ahead as a line which touches a semi-circular line at the top of the screen which relates the aircraft's current heading.

Ground beacons such as VORs are also displayed on the screen. And as stated earlier, the pilot can have the option of overlaying any weather that lies on the route. On some very modern aircraft such as the giant Airbus A380, the navigation display can also display the weather in a vertical mode as well as a plan view mode. This is especially valuable as it gives the pilot the heights of approaching cloud and allows him to choose whether he needs to fly above it or around it.

Navigation Display showing heading and the weather ahead

Although the initial cruise altitude is 36,000 feet, it is not likely to remain there for the duration of the flight. As fuel is burned off, it becomes more efficient for the aircraft to climb. There is a band of altitudes which the aircraft is designed to fly in. As long as the aircraft stays within this band and permission is granted to change altitude, then the aircraft will climb to maximise fuel efficiency. The rate of climb varies as to the type of aircraft but as a rough guide it may climb about 2,000 feet every two to four hours.

Depending on the length of the flight, the crew are also served refreshments and meals. A member of the cabin crew will enter the cockpit to take any orders. However, since the attacks on the Twin Towers in New York in 2001, the cockpit door stays locked. The days when passengers were welcomed into the cockpit during the cruise stage of a flight are sadly now past.

In fact, even before a cabin crew member is allowed into the cockpit they must use the intercom and speak to the pilot before being let in. On some new aircraft types, there are now two doors and a video camera showing that the person outside is who they say they are.

There is a story that the captain and first officer never have the same meal in case they may both get food poisoning. This is absolutely true. No chances are taken in this respect. In the very rare instance of a pilot falling ill, the other pilot is fully able and capable of flying the aircraft and making a safe landing. This is why the first officer is always a highly trained and qualified pilot and is given the responsibility of being the Pilot Flying on every other flight.

Communications

As far as most people are concerned, aircraft communications are carried out via radios. This is still true but gradually voice communications are being replaced by data link messages which are typed out and then sent to the current controller or are received from the ATC ground station. The system is known as Controller Pilot Data Link Communication or CPDLC.

The advantage of this system is that it can cut down on the amount of voice chatter over the various radio frequencies. At certain waypoints a number of aircraft may need to communicate with the one controller on duty at that ATC station. This quite often results in delays whilst you wait your turn to communicate your message and receive any clearances.

Lightweight headsets are used to communicate

If this sounds a bit like "texting" on your mobile phone, you are not very far from reality. However, to make life simpler, many of the requests and clearances which may be required have been standardised so that the crew only have to select the correct one from the range available and transmit it.

Of course the other advantage of this system is that it takes away the chance of mishearing the message. Although information is repeated to ensure it has been received correctly, mistakes have been made in the past. Now the message is in front of you on the screen or printed out.

This technique was first tried out in the South Pacific where communication stations are spread out over very long distances and the use of high frequency radios suffer from static and distortion. The result was positive and has now been introduced to many other remote parts of the globe.

However, there is one disadvantage; it can take a little while to receive a reply and to wait until it is printed out. Therefore pilots flying in the busier and more congested areas of Europe still prefer the immediacy of using VHF radios.

But the range of a VHF radio at altitude is only about 250 nautical miles. That isn't much good when crossing the Atlantic Ocean. Pilots would then have to use the high frequency (HF) radios which have a greater range. The present system of using the VHF when there are plenty of Air Traffic Service Units (ATSUs) around and utilising data link communications when flying over remote areas seems to work best for everyone concerned.

"Passengers prefer old captains

And young flight attendants…"

Anon

Chapter 7

Descent

Initial Descent

We are nearing the end of the cruise phase of the flight. In the passenger cabin any meals and drinks services will have been completed and the cabin crew will be passing through the aircraft in order to clear away any rubbish that has accumulated. Both for the cabin crew and the pilots, it is time to prepare to descend and eventually land at the destination airport.

All this time the Flight Management Computer (FMC) has been calculating where the optimum point to begin the descent should begin. As we approach it, a downward facing arrow has appeared on the route track line of the navigation display. This denotes the start of the descent and is often termed the "top of descent" mark.

The captain carries out the approach and landing briefing. Just as in the briefing before take-off, it lists the approach, the radio beacons which will be used, any special considerations and what the standard go-around procedure is should the aircraft not be able to land. The approach and landing plates will be produced. These are small charts showing the flight profile the aircraft must make in order to follow the correct route into the airport.

The crew also obtain the updated weather and information pertaining to the destination airport. When the briefing is complete, one of the pilots will make a call to the passengers to update them as to the estimated time of arrival, the local time so that they can reset their watches and most importantly for many of them, the expected weather conditions. The first officer will now begin the descent checklist.

At "Top of Descent" the engines are throttled back

Permission to descend is now requested and when granted, the throttles are pulled back to idle and the aircraft begins a controlled glide downwards. Rate of descent and speed are all controlled by the computer. It takes account of the prevailing winds and keeps the aircraft to its optimum rate of descent. It is likely that the actual winds will vary from the forecast so every now and again the passengers will notice the aircraft gently adjusting its descent and adding power in short bursts.

At the start of the flight, we referred to the planned route out of our starting airport as a SID which stands for Standard Instrument Departure. The aircraft is now following the approach and landing version of this which is called STAR. It stands for Standard Terminal Arrival Route.

As the aircraft descends the controllers will be clearing it to a specified altitude. When the aircraft is approaching that point, it is usually cleared to continue to the next altitude. If that clearance does not come then the aircraft must level out and wait for a further clearance to continue the descent. The aircraft will also be following a line of selected beacons as part of the standard approach profile. This means that the plane will be making turns as it approaches a beacon in order to head for the next one in line.

If the crew are lucky and conditions allow, the controller may give a clearance to fly direct to a beacon which is further along the line. This means that the aircraft can head directly for it and save some time. However this usually means that the aircraft will then be too high to hold the correct profile. The captain is left with one of two choices; he can either increase speed or he can select the air brakes to increase the descent rate.

By selecting these, small panels lift on the upper wings. These have the effect of disrupting the airflow and increasing drag causing the rate of descent to increase. The normal descent rate is about 2,500 feet per minute. As the speed brakes are deployed the descent rate will increase to about 5,000 feet per minute. When the aircraft is back on the correct height profile, they can be retracted back into the wing.

Initial Approach

As the aircraft passes through 10,000 feet the approach checklist will be called for and the "Fasten Seatbelts" sign will illuminate in the passenger cabin and everyone will be asked to take their seats. On the outside of the aircraft the bright landing lights will be switched on.

The aircraft continues to be cleared to lower levels. When it reaches the transition altitude for this particular area, the altimeter setting is changed to the current QNH value. If you recall from earlier, the QNH now gives the aircraft's height above sea-level. The captain soon calls for the Landing Checklist. Each item is confirmed by the crew and ticked off. However, when the flap selection item is reached, the checklist is temporarily halted. It will resume when it is time to begin deploying the flaps.

The flaps will be deployed in stages; Flaps 1, 2, 3 etc. It is important to understand that there is a maximum speed for each stage of flap deployment. Therefore it is vital that before flap is deployed, the speed of the aircraft is at or below this value.

The captain calls for "Flaps 1" and the first officer moves the flap lever to configuration 1 known as Config 1. The flaps roll out to their designated stage at the leading and trailing edges of the wings. The aircraft is now entering its final stages before landing.

"A good landing is one that you can walk away from.

A great landing is one where you can use the aeroplane again…"

Anon

Chapter 8

Landing

Final Approach

Each approach and landing procedure is different for each airport. That is why the crew will have a copy of the "Approach Plate" for that particular airport in front of them. However, it is likely the autopilot system will still be flying the plane and it will be faithfully following the procedure that has been input into the computer. The pilots will be checking and cross-checking the numbers to make sure that all is well.

In order to set itself up in the correct position to make a final approach to land, the aircraft is heading towards a beacon which is termed the Initial Approach Fix (IAF). When overhead the beacon and at the particular stated height, the aircraft will then turn in accordance with the procedure. In this example, we will assume that our turn is taking us onto the final approach to our landing runway.

At around this point, the radio altimeters may come into operation. These work by bouncing radio signals off the ground and back to the aircraft. They are extremely accurate and are used when the aircraft is low. The air traffic controller calls to clear the aircraft to land on the designated runway. The first officer repeats the clearance and the aircraft is now looking for the Final Approach Fix (FAF). This is a beacon which for this procedure will bring the Instrument Landing System (ILS) into play. When established on the ILS, the aircraft will make its final descent for a landing.

Crew preparing to land

The Approach Plate is on the control column

Landing

The autopilot is still enabled and is now looking for the Final Approach Fix and then to "capture" the ILS. There is a Distance Measuring Instrument, called a DME which is reading out the distance to the FAF. As it reaches it, the crew notice that the ILS is coming in. When the ILS is captured, it means that the aircraft is now lined up with the runway in use and is at a set height and stated distance from the threshold of the runway. It can now descend at a given rate which will bring it in to a landing.

At this point, the captain decides to take over and manually fly the aircraft in for its landing. He presses the autopilot disconnect button on the control column. Then he calls for "Flap 2" and the flaps deploy further. The speed of the aircraft drops to a set figure and the captain calls for the undercarriage to be lowered. The first officer pulls the undercarriage lever down and waits until all three green lights are illuminated indicating the wheels are down and locked. The order for "Flaps 3" follows.

The aircraft begins its final descent towards the runway. On the Primary Flight Display the glideslope is displayed and the captain faithfully follows the slope down. He calls for "Full Flaps" and the flaps move to their final position of full deployment. The first officer is now able to complete the Landing Checklist.

As the aircraft reaches the decision altitude, the captain confirms he has the runway in sight and will fly the plane visually from this point. The auto-thrust is left on in order not to fall below the safe minimum speed. If there were a sudden change in wind direction or speed, it could have the effect of bringing the aircraft's speed to near what is required for a safe approach.

Full Flap – Landing Gear Down – Finals to Land

The synthesised voice from the radio altimeter calls out the height of the aircraft above the ground. It will call out the height every 100 feet below 300 feet and when the aircraft reaches 50 feet, it will call out every 10 feet. As the aircraft descends to the 50 feet mark, the captain begins to flare the aircraft by easing the control column back. This has the effect of slowing the rate of descent and raising the nose in order to let the main wheels touch the runway first.

Main wheels touch first on landing

The crew then hear another synthesised voice command saying "Retard." This tells the pilot to bring the throttles back from their climb (CL) position into the idle position. The action also causes the auto-thrust to disengage. The captain holds the aircraft just off whilst it gently sinks the last remaining feet onto the runway. The captain then lowers the nose until the nose-wheel makes contact with the runway.

The speed brakes deploy automatically to cut any lift that might be present and to help with the braking. The level of braking can be set by the pilot before touching down. All passengers are aware of the sudden increase in noise levels and the strong feeling of slowing up that happens just after landing. This is due to another system of braking; reverse thrust. The engines are able to reverse the direction of thrust which has a strong braking effect on the aircraft. At slower speeds they are disconnected and normal braking takes over.

When the aircraft has slowed sufficiently, it will turn off the runway onto one of the designated taxiways and head towards its stand. After Landing Checks are now carried out. The flaps are recovered, the auxiliary power unit is turned on and other non-essential items are turned off. The first officer will have retuned the radio to the ground controller's frequency who will guide them to the stand.

Arrival and Deplaning

As the aircraft approaches its stand, the pilot makes a call to the cabin crew of "Doors to manual." This is the order to disarm the doors so that the automatic deployment of the slides cannot occur. In the cockpit, the crew bring the aircraft to a halt at the designated stand. Air conditioning is changed over to the APU, other lights such as the seat belt signs are turned off and other systems are cancelled. The engines can now be shut down.

During this time a ground engineer informs the captain via the intercom that the wheels chocks are now in place and he can release the parking brake. The Shut Down checklist is carried out and the final paperwork is completed.

As the crew gather up their personal things, the responsibility of the aircraft moves to the ground engineer. If the plane is in transit mode he or she will now have about two hours to prepare the aircraft for a new crew and destination. Airliners do not make any money when they are sat on the ground. So it is in the airline's interests to get each aircraft ready for its next job as quickly as possible.

The passengers will now have departed or "deplaned" the aircraft and will be heading for immigration, luggage retrieval and customs before setting off from the airport.

Air travel is becoming more and more popular and many more people are experiencing what it is like to travel across the world in only a relatively few hours. But for many, it is an alien feeling and not knowing what is really going on out of sight does not make things easier. However, I hope that this book has gone some way in helping to clear up some of the questions many passengers would like to ask the pilot. When you know what is going on at every stage of a flight, you can relax and enjoy the whole experience a lot more.

Have many more happy and enjoyable flights.

"We have a perfect record in aviation.

We never left one up there…"

Anon

Chapter 9

Aircraft Data

Airliners vary in size and type. They may have 2, 3 or 4 engines. Their range may be a few thousand miles to almost halfway across the world. The following data pages list some of the more common airliners you are likely to fly on your travels.

For the most part you are likely to encounter two aircraft manufacturers, Airbus and Boeing. Airbus is a European company owned by a number of countries and the Boeing Aircraft Corporation is American. In addition there are many other companies who build aircraft but they are, at the moment, on a much smaller scale.

The selection includes two short to medium range aircraft:

Airbus A-320

Boeing 737-800.

These are joined by two long-haul aircraft:

Airbus A-380 Super-Jumbo

Boeing 747-400.

The data figures can vary with the type of operation the aircraft is designed to do, so the following numbers have been averaged out to be as accurate as possible.

Airbus A-320

Airbus A-320

Length: 37.57 m

Wingspan: 34.09 m

Engines: 2 CFM 56-5A1 turbofans

Max Speed: 454 knots

Range: 2615 nautical miles

Max Take-Off Weight: 73,500 kg

Aircrew: 2 pilots

Passengers: 179

Airbus A-380

Airbus A-380

Length: 72.75 m

Wingspan: 79.8 m

Engines: 4 Rolls-Royce Trent 900

Max Speed: Mach 0.85

Range: 5,600 nautical miles

Max Take-Off Weight: 560,000 kg

Aircrew: 2 pilots

Passengers: 555

Boeing 737-800

Boeing 737

Length: 39.47 m

Wingspan: 34.31 m

Engines: 2 CFM 56-7B24

Max Speed: Mach 0.785

Range: 1990 nautical miles

Max Take-Off Weight: 70,535 kg

Aircrew: 2 pilots

Passengers: 177

Boeing 747-400

Boeing 747

Length: 70.67 m

Wingspan: 64.44 m

Engines: 4 Rolls-Royce RB-211

Max Speed: 490 knots

Range: 7,284 nautical miles

Max Take-Off Weight: 362,878 kg

Aircrew: 2 pilots

Passengers: 416

Further Information

For further information about the author, go to

www.johnpullenwriter.com

For further information and DVDs about flying, go to;-

www.pilottrainingdvds.com

Other Books by the same Author

Non-Fiction

Aviation Series

How to Fly a Plane

How to Fly an Airliner

The Private Pilot Flying Course Part 1

The Private Pilot Flying Course Part 2

The Private Pilot Skill Test

The Flight Pilot Radio Manual

The Flight Pilot Instrument Rating Flying Course Part 1

The Flight Pilot Instrument Rating Flying Course Part 2

Medical Series

Hypnotherapy

Stop Smoking

Being Happy

History Series

Secret London Churches

Secret London Places

Secret Bloody London

Flying the Dream

Fiction

Dragon's Claw

Dark Angel

Rogue Knight

All available through Createspace & Amazon

Search "John Pullen" on

www.createspace.com or www.amazon.co.uk

Printed in Great Britain
by Amazon